WET SIDEWALKS

Poems Found While Out Walking In The World

by Tom Typinski

TOM TYPINSKI

ISBN: 978-0-9907776-5-6
ISBN-13:978-0-9907776-5-6

DEDICATION

TO WRITING;
IT BROUGHT ME HERE, IT TAKES ME BACK

TABLE OF CONTENTS

<u>SUNSET, BEACHED</u>

Ahh muse.
I sent you out for a walk
my friend; My friend,
I saw you rolling in the sand;
saw the crystals stick to
your back and reflect
the sunlight like flint.

And when I asked if I
could lend a hand
you threw sand and
said, "be gone."

You said, "you fool, I
lay here not to hide nor
beg but to work the
scales, to cleanse –
this sand makes smooth
the edges I used
as tools for your defense.
You come to me after prayerful
laments like I hold
your secrets –
"please, please…understand!"
but Muse means "you,"
means "me and you's." You
see, you stupid fool?
You hold your cards,

you hold your keys,
not me, nor any
disguise you use.
Recognize me –
the me of your eyes."
And with that she
vanished –
"Poof!"

I fell to my knees,
sifting granules, seeking her
truth, examining each grain
of my youth. I built
fortresses, dug holes,
watched the water
pound and unfold
until my senses returned
to me. I breathed the salt
and the smoke but yet
no one else spoke so I
left with what I
came with –
Me.

ROSARY

It starts in a circle
always a circle because
It always comes back

on huddled knees
hiding the wind
starting field fires
just to watch things burn

You steal Daddy's Kools
and gather, coughing suavely
-SHARING-
burning weed and speed, swearing
"I will if you will"
-SHARING-
experiments while tied
to Ma's rosary beads
between bong hits and Boone's Farm
you find clarity
-SHARING-
ideas of escape, dreams

"Ring the Rosary" comes
"Spin the Bottle" comes
pass the bottle
comes puke

passed out and drug home on the shoulders
of those you're sharing for support
hiding war stories and sadness and defeat
because you all
-SHARED-
the same set of parents

You climb to the bottom through
"Burning Rings of Fire"
jumping through hoops
to please everyone but you
regardless the brilliance
or foolishness shown

The "Rosary of Experience"
played one bead at a time
hyena-laughing at the fun in nothing,
moon-howling, sun-sitting,
tear-drenched in the rain
so friends can't see the epiphanies you cry

The pain and pleasure blurr until that circle
of an Angel's eyes form two-into-one
and you're seated
at a round table of strangers
- SHARING -
how every bead was exactly necessary
and how you now realize it
but are no longer afraid of it
simply because some circle of friendship
appeared to finally acknowledge your spirit

You end praying
ever-thankful for each and every bead
of every seed planted
that made you be you and me be me.

LOVE, LONELINESS

When you're up all night
watching movies with the sound off

When you walk in silence
talking monotones

When you're breakfast says nothing
and you speak to the cat

When your mind goes to sleep
and you don't care where it's at

You're in the stages of loneliness
and only love can bring you back.

<u>BARTER</u>

The air is of sex.
Every eye wanders.
Every hip invites.
Women and men on
the see-saw of small town,
balanced between "who's sleeping with,"
and "who's left."

The fiery glances,
the flexing limbs screaming for attention;
lonely, where everyone pretends not to be.
Lonely; the push-pull of invitation,
acceptance, rejection in a breath;
wanting only to be loved
but letting love be the only thing they won't give.

A million bucks in endowments
but the doctor couldn't create a smile,
just a grim, smug scowl shouting "I've got it all"
while the heart's aura can't hide the hole inside
or the memory of tomorrow.

"..looking for love in a looking glass world is pretty hard to find."

Whereas, on this side of town,
the air is of garages and attics and old sweaters.
It says, "cheap, cheap, cheap…" from the haggard hair
to the flip-flopped feet.
The wanna-be's are has-beens

and the old money left a trail of receipts
as deep as their worn riding boots and dirty Nike's.
Girth has replaced height in stature
while intelligence buys deception in managing their piece.
The town rules with weakness
despite the atheleisurely jogging moms
in pants stretched beyond their purpose,
about to burst from the strain of "buns of meals."

Still, they preen in mirrors that search for their best side;
pretending not to hide in expenditures beyond their rent,
their scent an expensive stench hiding last night's breath;
an air of "where we were…and who we were seen by… and with";
precedes their knees bent to chairs uneasily holding them,
bartering for attention, recognition, temporary
acceptance in false speeches meant to impress.

<u>A PRAYER FOR '89</u>

Let peace be within your heart
let it start with love
Let it forever be the thing which
inspires you to begin
to show affection for even one and everyone

What this world needs is to slow down
to show what is meaningful
instead of meander like
so many others in the quagmire
of defining life and it's challenges

To live and be better
to see through the letters
of "Thank you" or "Love you"
to what really means "need you."
The plea of forgiveness is
the seed of deliverance

We all want, need and plea
but what we get is rarely seen
in the example for progeny
We are instruments in future tense

We suffer so our children
will be free of the strife
that envelopes you and I
We are a force of love, of defense
against anything resembling penance.

We've prayed enough
We've suffered the crumbs of fate
now we have love;
now we have something
to rely upon.

BLUE

Blue
Midnight blue like the sky a.m.
when the stars hang like punctured holes
unmoving like dandruff in the
deep like a thought holding your mind
hostage, mesmerizing like hypnosis
or a fond memory of a childhood shortfalling

Intelligent and intellectual, deep and
everpresent as dark as black but no
evil connotations because of its sparkle
and luster of hope because blue means
forgiveness as well as sadness and happiness
like a blue sky over Siesta Key or sea of
"Tidy Bowl" Maui, the navy of a uniform
and uniform in it's breadth, unflagging,
meaningful, devotion to depth and intellect
The blue of a Blue-black stallion
seen only with the direct, correct
reflection of sunlight or moonlight
as he turns away running, thundering
into the night, into the day
so unafraid because to run is his job,
his will and his destiny, undirected,
unrestricted, unheeded and not needing to
abide to rules governing humans – freedom.
It takes you. It fills you like a
thirst-quenching gorge after a day's dehydration

As blue as the sea gets,
it always is clear when picked up in hand.
It's its own mystery.
Clear blue.
It's
me.

<u>DAD</u>

He waved as I went by
walking fast toward me
then relinquishing his steps
as he saw my momentum
the roar of my creaking mufflers
drowned his "Hey."
I know I crushed him by not stopping by
I know each morning
as I turn over the dinosaur
en route to work
he cries inside
for his son to stop, to say hi,
to explain to him why
I drive by past my past
over the years of arguments
and instructions and demands.

I can't stand what I'm doing
any more than what they said
My notion of them is "old"
and the pity swells me, for the way
I see "them" in a future where they
still don't understand for all their lecturing
it's them who've never learned
who haven't set free that seed
which is love. If they don't see me
How do I believe in them?

FRICTION

The feel of a pen
a tire on a road
music when it harmonizes
a physical expelling of toxins
a pull of gravity eastward
as the page falls below
cascading meaning, meandering,
trickling and crashing
thunderous across the vast
white plains of thought

A flow of swirling sensation
from head to toe
trancelike in its demands,
leading, daring, comparing
whim to inspiration,
a learning curve of life
measured in sentences.

Solidified in time as remembrance,
experience leaves to follow the flow:
up, across, with friction, with tumult
crumbling emotions locked in vaults.

WET SEPTEMBER

September's wet, misty fog
rolled stagnate as the car thrust into the gray,
fast and blind like an amusement ride
racing to outdistance the headlights beyond

Hurled forward like a boy running
under fresh covers Mother flips,
a "tidal wave" of clothesline scent,
and love in the suppleness she seals in
each night, each sheet, each bed.

The mist, its own undoing;
timeless, unhindered, unmoved
by the currents stirred of rushing fenders,
bumpers pushing with illuminated grins;
it hangs unwavered, strolling its grey ghost shadow
across land and kid and metal
settling like the clammy hand of unfamiliar lovers,
forced to find the reality of the dark.

<u>GRAY CITY</u>

The pavement pulls gray Camaros
of gray-suited young men
whose only wish is to wear
a blue suit and drive a blue Lincoln, "just like Dad."

Speedy red Fieros with their fiery female drivers
zooming obliviously through lanes while
they look only at their cigarette tip and lipstick.

The poet in the Pinto laughs
leaning hard and squinting,
trying to catch her glimpse
but only sees the red flash
of her sarcastic laugh
lifting his blue mood.

She's gone for good
but his imagination
holds the resolution.

<u>ADVENTUROUS MIND</u>

He was walking all alone,
till he found a stick
with a crook in it.

He skied the slopes of Kilimanjaro,
became a blind man probing the soil,
transformed, and stormed a gladiator with a lance,
stick-handled past the Soviets,
and played the xylophone fence.

The stick broke,
he moped, then sotto-spoke,
"I'm tired. It's late.
I'm galloping home to bed."

<u>DON'T ASK</u>

Can the writer
write too many words
Can the artist draw
too many lines
Does the speech slowly
turn absurd
Does the picture blur
from years of time
Will a paragraph or
simple sentence suffice
as long as it's voice
reads concise
Will a silhouette
convey the meaning
Enough to show the artists' dreaming

No need to ask,
when someone's hand
Acts as a mask
and takes a stand.

<u>ONE EYE OPEN</u>

With only one eye open
day clear, still, welcoming
regretfully remembering Franklin's forte
"Early to rise" with squeaking knees
as I bend to my seat
Thoughts oppressive
"why me?"
Traveling with speeders, 7:15;
So many. Such hurried
nosepicking businessmen
heading for cities with
"done" as a destiny.

AS BAD AS IT LOOKS

Cockamamy place, Key West
Called West when it's Southern and dips to the east
A haven of heathens washed up on it's reefs
lost souls, boy lovers, lonely women, Cuban kids,
awash in the poverty
of freedom only America gives.

Addicts, Winos, Fags, Loners, piano-toothed smiles in the sun;
dirtbag dealers, daylight traders of pirated goods
to make the misfits more alienated,
out of touch, obscured from view.

Small shops and small minds full of small ideas
and entitled views of "give me this, I'll take that"
"you got ripped," "you got jewed," so did you;
as sandals smack pavement telling stories
of discontented, misplaced opportunity,
ignoring the obvious clue of laziness.

DRIZZLE, DRAZZLE, DRUZZLE, DRONE

Driving the drizzly highway
Rush hour time
At exactly four ten
when men
pick their noses to
their hearts content
halfway between the
etiquette of office
and role modeling
of home.
Alone
on their own,
to pick and choose and choose and pick
and chew.

TIME (7-86)

There was a time when time meant nothing to me
where days lay unending, spinning hours of carefree reverie;
and baseball or bikes were the major concerns,
money was unnecessary, friendships earned.

Each day I'd learn of something new in the fields
new bugs to handle, new stones to wield
the tenderness of the grass on my back
was affection enough, and love, yes love,
came in forms of home runs and touchdowns
jelly sandwiches and dogs;
puddles of mud leant amazing discoveries
and trees were the secrets of my hiding.

The breadth of the sunshine and the sting of snow
melted deep memories, aglow
in the aftermath of a bed warm with covers of my own.
The next morning's sun shone through the slit of my shade
to tell me another day was there;
though all was a challenge, I welcomed the sun
because there was never fear of failure
with daylight as my measure.
Time dates, it sits on my shoulders
telling me there's more to do;
responsibility's preying and
my mind makes excuses while yesterdays muses
cast absentee amusements
yet, in my eyes, I see the fields, hear the bees,
smell the grass laying lodged in my past.

<u>LIMERICK 158</u>

There once was a squirrel

In chi town

Who danced the lambada

Unclothed

With nuts in his pockets

And scraps in his jowls

He took home the girl

In a towel.

<u>MIAMIAMAZED</u>

Cuban waiters in a German brewery
Spaniards reading English
talking Gibberish
at bistro café internationale.

More cops per square foot
than donut shops have donuts
Utility belted bat men
walk-talking for crooks
Where men tell Cubans
where to stand, sit or walk
Drinking draught between
bustings on the sidewalk.

Grinning grannys
with skinny fannies
nothing really to watch
Little ghetto, Little Cuba
service rendered with "what?"
Wanderers walking, wasting
days at the mall
unfunded shoppers browsing
window stuffed dolls.

<u>PURPOSE</u>

Waking is the first prayer to carry me from bed to breakfast.
He is on my mind and in my voice as I work, play, wait for the
day to witness how I can serve.

Whatever it takes and
No matter how long
In any way it comes out
I'll wait.
I'll write it out.
In any form
metamorphosing through strong chains
tied only to Posterity.
I'll write it out.
I'll wait.
In any way it comes out
No matter how long
and whatever it takes.

<u>Every Night I Just Gotta Get Out</u>

Just want to step out of my head
No feelings left
no words to be said
Just want to get out of my head
Because the dreaded thing has
gotten all crammed
Just want to leave don't want to think
on my own I've had enough thoughts
Now just leave me alone
No drugs or sex to lead where
I want to be
Just want to get out of
inside of me
Maybe a fast lane with a
car on my ass
90 per hour won't even seem fast
I want to drive so far I'll
never look back
So tired I wont stop until I crack
not escaping life
not seeking death
not self pity
I just want a rest
I'm so sick of taking test after test
I think a break from me would
do me best.

POTPOURRI (dream of life)

A feeling like someone is pushing against my face, under my chin, trying to keep me away from this paper, this notebook, this pen. A vise has me by the head and as the skull crushes in there's a library of words stacked, untapped, to my ears. I dig for the right one dig and dig and dig but they just slide off each other stacking up to naught and I'm lost in the labyrinth of memory, a cage with spikes and barbs beside softest down.The sharp spears seem to leap at me, knowing they don't move as I nestle and nuzzle in the feather-bed warmth of a coma immune to thought and purpose reaching, pulling, wanting for all that lay within arms reach. A ring is my handle, another, a foothold. I climb through the tunnel of my mind, I climb for days, there is nothing to find, except the next ring which teases as I grasp, its coolness not budging beneath my clasp. A ring forms in my other hand as the walls split, I stand with arms outstretched in an iron cross, the floor drops and I gasp for breath, the vacuum pulling air like an amusement park Rotor Ride. Arms stretched straight, my hands sweat, my grip slips ever so slightly. My shoulders ache and the pain runs down my triceps to my elbows and wrists making me one with the rings I hold in my hands.The pain goes away, my chin leans to the sky and I"m gone -

-UP-

I'm flying, the scenery rushing past as I laugh like a child thrown high from his father's hands, ascending, always ascending, never to land. The rings turn to keys as my body eases into flight, I float without effort, without pain, without thought. This feeling can never be bought. I float through doors, across water, the keys drop free, weighing my hands with electricity which tingles and stuns me to reverie, making me giddy. I'm free. I reach overhead as the sky starts to darken as stars light streets hushed above and around me, each its own avenue, each with a view of a scene that is happy and true: small movies I look in on, spinning tales of me and of you, that are told over and over again, reruns in the skies which defy time by infiniteness, never to cease but to link end to end; though I don't recognize anyone in those skies, I know each have/ are living my identical lives.The stars are sidewalks which push when I step, launching me forward, hurling me comedically like Chaplin when the frames ran too fast. I cartwheel on my stroll like spokes minus wheels, a pinwheel of flesh; and as I spin I see one thing, the face of - not me - my other side, my better half that's young and not yet destructed, worn, bruised or bleeding. It is the scepter, she, the mother-lover-wife who bore my sons and made bearable my life by adding laughter and sharing and the one-to-one bond, making both of us fuller, both complete in their dimension by adding that mystery plane of love. Her light blinds me, her eyes guide me through this difficult maze, as if she travelled it daily. I follow, pulled by her aura, swept in her grace that traces the outline of what she is to be if I am ever complete, and "I will be complete" she says to me.The stars fall, sidewalks crumble, rings ping from their hold as we're left in all grayness as far as sight stretches yet happiness here reigns supreme.We are not scared, we don't even flinch as our hands join together in a circle round our children who dance and sing music and color our world; energy to me from her and verse vice, the children a turbine of energy as they swirl yellows, reds, greens and blues on the landscape of our imagination; completely free through our trust to be what the will created, men and women shining brilliantly; passing on trinkets through time because they know no lies and their world which we've created is magnificent no matter what ruins it lays amongst. Like planets we glow in our unique auras keeping distinct yet close spreading warmth and kindness to the ends of the skies, lands and seas - always free, always committed to oneself, Thee. The dream wakes me gently to the breeze of beginning where each day offers new ways of seeing the meaning of the simple things, the beauty of life above mundane. Life on earth should never be the same while conformity rules us, that's how they school us and what little mind we're left with is so much less than open when compared to the vast scope of what really is offered as a mortal on this planet. People resolve to be cramped, I cannot stand it; cramped for time, for space, for money, for breath, each moment lasting eons stretching out directionless; The Power of Positive Thinking as Peale pronounced is simply the ability to see both sides at once, then to choose with discretion the route you've resolved, sticking to it, never wandering, picking bits to help along; but leaving the empty furniture at home. I roam and I seek yet I'm still so meek to leave the furniture and be on my way.

<u>REARVIEW MIRROR</u>

Why look back?
What's in a rearview mirror
when the road's rolling under you?
Just excuses for why you are and
regrets over where you should have been.
Living it over's not possible
Thinking about it, sometimes unbearable
but still there's memories of those
friends you thought so dear and those
precious events that were so dramatic
when now only bits and fragments of
worked-over stories linger.
"Remember the time…"
But what about tomorrow?
Are those happy, good moments over or
are more to come?
What brings that hard earned happiness
that used to come so easy and nonchalant?
I'll tell my sons there's always more,
that one must give.
The only secret to life!
LIVE

SOCIAL CONTACTS:

www.TomTypinski.com
Facebook: Tom Typinski
YouTube: Tom Typinski
Instagram: Mr._Tom_Typinski
Twitter:@TomTypinski
LinkedIn: Tom Typinski